A Nip around the World
the diary
of
a whisky salesman

Malcolm Greenwood

Argyll
publishing

First published 1995
Argyll Publishing
Glendaruel
Argyll PA22 3AE
Scotland

British Library Cataloguing-in-Publication Data.
A catalogue record for this book is available from the British Library.

ISBN 1 874640 96 3

Origination
Cordfall Ltd, Glasgow

Printing
BPC Paulton Books Limited

for mother and father

Introduction

For a living, I sell Scotch whisky at home and abroad. It may sound a bit corny but I do love travel and meeting people.

My travels take me round the UK, Europe, the Far East and the United States. I do take my sales very seriously and I believe I do my job in a professional way. But during my 'field trips' I often find myself in very funny situations.

I am not one to deal in gossip, or to talk shop in my

local, but I've found that if something funny happens to me during my travels, I can usually raise a laugh or two.

Friends have encouraged me to put pen to paper and share some of these stories further. *A Nip around the World* is the result.

There have been many books written on travel and selling, but I believe that this one takes a look at these subjects in a way which is unique — it is, after all, made up of my individual experiences. The book is written in the form of a diary and it covers the twelve months of a typical year.

If in the course of writing I have caused anyone embarrassment, then please forgive me. It is not intentional. I thank you, the reader, for buying the book. I sincerely hope it gives you as much pleasure as I had writing it. Read on, and as they say in the USA, enjoy!

Malcolm Greenwood
August 1995

Swiss Chocolate

G rindelwald must be one of the most beautiful Alpine retreats on earth. Lying in the shadows of the Eiger, it is simply breathtaking. It is no wonder they make movies here!

I arrived late at night at the hotel Chalet Caprice, a very traditional wooden Swiss chalet with log fires burning, St Bernard dogs, cow bells and warmness.

My bedroom was pine clad, a little over-hot. A huge bed filled the room. The duvet was pure white as were the crispen sheets. I decided to open the skylight and looked up and up at the colossal mountain. It loomed overhead against an inky blue sky, the air was pure and frosty.

A little light like a star, twinkled overhead. This was the 'Window' of the Eiger, a vent duct carved out of rock. You can look down from here, to what appears an eternity, if you dare! The North face.

This was my first trip to Switzerland and the event was a sponsorship of a curling competition. I was determined to be a professional, my boss being a personal friend of the hotel owner.

As a company we provide whisky for the Glenfarclas 'Barrel' (now in its fifteenth year). This is a bonspiel curling competition on ice, very jovial and friendly. It creates much goodwill which is reflected in the sales for that area.

Throughout the day-long competition malt whisky is provided free of charge 'from the barrel' to the players' preference. It could be described as a bit boozy!

To conclude the day a fondue meal is provided courtesy of the Chalet Caprice. The Swiss take their fondues seriously. Huge amounts of Gruyère cheese, and lashings of Kirsch.

Max, a competitor and organiser of the event took me to one side. Obviously concerned, he introduced me to the 'dangers' of fondue. The problem with filling your face with molten cheese and bread, is that if you wash it down with chilled beer, the cheese reconstitutes itself into 'balls' which form in your tummy.

This has dire effects on your digestive system. It has been known to be fatal, at best chronic diarrhoea results.

To remedy the beer problem Max suggested a liberal dowsing of schnapps, "to break up the cheese you understand". I felt this could be a wind-up. Max is cordially known as Mad Max locally!

The evening passed very pleasantly indeed. I found the company warm and friendly and was much taken by the hospitality. On the conclusion of that misty night I was presented with colourful wall posters of the area, a Swiss pocket knife and the most enormous box of Suchard chocolates I have ever seen.

I retired to my room via a small passageway after much hand shaking, hugs and embraces. A huge St Bernard called Tiny drooled on my hand, but its affections were more directed to what I was carrying. My room was delightful. The bed enticing.

I lay back under the light weight but full togged

duvet. The day had been glorious, the schnapps wonderful. All was well.

I suddenly felt a little peckish. The pretty box of chocolates were at hand. Just one I thought! Propped on my chest I opened the box. And what a glorious sight.

I did not realise at first the extent of the gift. Beautiful liquor filled chocolates, all in rows categorised by regions. My selection began. Unfortunately at this stage 'fatigue' took over and I drifted off to sleep.

Horror met me next morning! The duvet and sheets were running brown.

I thought immediately of the warnings from Max about 'fondue side effects'. But no, I had tossed and turned all night, my companion being the tray of now molten chocolates.

Explain that to the hotelier. Swiss are so discreet.

A Nip around the World

The Wall, Berlin 1989

I always remember this city with great embarrassment. Perhaps you know the feeling when all you want in the world is for a trap door to open up beneath you and simply whisk you away?

We were working in Berlin at the time the wall was coming down. Brightly coloured chunks of concrete were being sold everywhere. An historical and hysterical moment.

We were to be conducting a sales promotion within the flagship store KaDeWae (a bit like Harrods). The idea was to offer a free 'tasting' of our whisky to potential customers, and to encourage them to buy. Most stores and duty-free outlets welcome this activity. It costs them nothing and increases their sales, and it gives your product some 'limelight'.

My journey had originated in Basle. The train I was waiting for, was coming from Milan. Then it would travel on through Eastern Germany and on to Moscow.

How romantic I thought, as I stood on the platform. For days I had built up in my mind an Orient Express illusion.

A lavish steam locomotive with Pullman carriages, a stylish restaurant car, panelled in dark mahogany, lit by polished brass lights and wrapped in rich purple velvet curtains. Smoke from black Russian cigarettes would hang lightly in the air, and spies would talk in hushed voices.

The nightcap of warming brandy, the soothing melody playing softly in the background, against the chatter of heavy wheels on cold steel rails. All the while, gazing out at frosty moonlit landscapes. Starched and crisp cotton sheets, turned down, a complimentary milk chocolate. Occasionally to be startled by the brisk sharp scream of a steam whistle as the train thundered through long dark tunnels and on into the night. Trickety trick, trickety trick . . .

What a dreamer, Malcolm! A very dirty diesel freight train pulled in. Attached as if in an afterthought were four carriages. The spell was broken.

My heart lifted momentarily at observing the first of these carriages. You could not see through the glass properly for condensation, but hanging inside, pendant-style were little communist flags in bright red and gold.

Adventure at last! I thought, but no, this carriage had been locked off.

I shook hands enthusiastically with Phillipe, our importer in Switzerland, and climbed aboard.

This was the dirtiest and most smelly train I have ever been on. If it had been a building, it would have been condemned. It oozed filth. All the seating was threadbare and shone in greasy stains.

It looked as if someone had gone mad with a sugar shaker. Except that the sugar was dandruff. Balls of dirty hair were caught in the seat recesses. I dared not look at the floor.

Each compartment 'slept' six persons, with three folding down bunks on each side. You were therefore obliged to lie down, God forbid, should your comrades above wish to turn in for the night.

I imagined the clouds of old hair and dandruff coming drifting down to my bottom bunk. They called , them 'couchettes' — pronounced 'cowsheds' or 'coo shit'. Quite appropriate really.

In short if two people from each side wanted to go to sleep, then the whole bloody lot·of us would have to go to bed. Very democratic.

Oh well, at least there will be a buffet car, I thought. I could stay up late, have a nice dinner, some wine, and then by that time, not care much anyway.

I had in any event worked out the practicalities of using my large overcoat as a barrier between me and those dreadful bunks. Things were starting to look rosier as the train pulled out, and I went in search of food.

There was no buffet car. The only catering provided was that prepared by a Turkish gentleman who blended chameleon-like with his surroundings.

His *piece de resistance* was cooked over a very ancient and smoky paraffin stove.

His gastronomic talents had progressed to warming up frankfurter sausages in their brine. Cleverly, he did not even require a pot. He simply cut open the large catering tin and placed it directly over the flame. No, I will never again grumble at British Rail sandwiches.

In actual fact, my only companion in the 'cowshit' was a very fat middle aged Polish woman. She exchanged no pleasantries at all, not even a 'good-night'. But Christ, could she fart!

Dozing off eventually, in what by now was a very stale atmosphere, we were to be rudely awakened by East German officials checking passports. Berlin at that time was still an enclave within communist Germany, but only just.

I arrived knackered. It was 7.00am and freezing cold on that January morning. I felt like a refugee. Certainly not a 'Public Relations Officer'. Definitely not a 'Brand Ambassador'.

Bernie McGee, our importer in Germany at the time, met me heartily. He comes from Edinburgh and is married to a lovely German woman. A very jolly man, bubbling with enthusiasm. We made our way back to his apartment. Beastie, his wife, had prepared the most scrumptious Scottish breakfast, with lashings of strong, piping hot coffee. Nectar.

Bernie began to explain our programme for the next two days. We were to be conducting the in-store promotion in conjunction with 'Food and Drink from Britain'. This organisation is funded by the UK government and is affiliated to the Department of Agriculture. Its aim is to promote British products in this sector, overseas.

Thus there was much Union Jack bunting everywhere. Many other Scottish firms were represented. Bernie had done all the preparations the previous day and our stand sparkled. So all we had to do was don our kilts and set off. We arrived at 9.30am.

Our neighbours were Moet and Chandon and Budweiser (the original Czech variety). It is simply the best beer I have ever tasted. There was much 'Guten Morgens'.

The store itself smacked of affluence. It was an Aladdin's cave of luxury goods. This of course was at the time the wall was coming down.

By lunchtime the store was packed, mostly with East Germans. They stood out from their compatriots. As different as chalk and cheese. Trabbants (trabbies) to Mercedes.

They reminded me of children at Christmas, all starry-eyed, innocent in some strange way. Some expressions were of utter dejection, despair. As if they had just learned of a closely guarded secret. Of course they just had.

None of these people could afford anything. They could look but not touch. Sickening really, to observe. I felt a bit ashamed.

One young man unnerved me in his defiant and proud stare, as if saying, "the East will come and take its share". A shiver ran down my spine.

To bring a bit of zest to our Scottish stand we had enlisted the services of a piper from the Irish Guards. His repertoire flourished as we duly 'watered' him. This attracted much interest and curiosity. The promotion was an outstanding success.

With much gusto, farewells and beers were exchanged with our Czech friends and then Bernie and I went to relax in one of the many Irish bars in the city.

My Saturday was a day off for sightseeing and Bernie proved the most courteous guide. I learned more of his renouned style, and his hard neck. No, we did not simply visit the Brandenburg Gate, but had a picnic just beyond it, on the East German side, and bang in front of the Russian Embassy! This would have been unthinkable even one month before, and we would probably still be in jail if we had attempted it.

The picnic was 'the works', with wicker basket, china cups, huge napkins and slabs of paté sandwiches. The hip flask was produced.

I felt a little uneasy, as we observed the young Russian soldiers nearby, goose-stepping in heavy grey coats and polished knee length boots in front of an eternal flame. Someone told me recently that these coats are produced in Aberdeen!

Bernie pointed to a large grassy mound a few hundred metres away. He explained that underneath was Hitler's bunker and how the Russians had discovered his half burned body when they entered the city in 1945. To discover further macabre details when entering.

It was sealed off with concrete blocks, not long afterwards. We stood in the shadows of the magnificent Brandenburg Gate, with its proud eagles and chariots still pockmarked from artillery fire. A memorable and haunting experience.

Sunday arrived and Bernie, Beastie and his two
children picked me up from my hotel. We were to have
lunch at the Berlin Officers Club. I instinctively felt
uncomfortable and thought that this family was definitely
overdressed for what I had assumed would be a normal
Sunday lunch.

The British army at that time was getting ready to
leave, in a big way, but there was a decidedly jubilant
atmosphere as we entered the Club.

They were having a 'theme' lunch and Russia was
the flavour! We were welcomed and toasted with very
cold and very neat vodka, and Oh yes, it had to go down
in one. An orchestra was playing sweetly, 'Lara's theme'
from the film, *Dr Zhivago*. I noticed many cocktail dresses
and bow ties. I cringed a bit and although wearing a
reasonable wool suit, I still felt Marks & Spencer lit in
neon on my back. Bernie and I had provided the whisky
for the after lunch drink. We mingled.

The whole place had a wonderful imperial style,
with some very beautiful military flags from bygone
battles. Silver cups and trophies glistened. The British
Ambassador for Berlin was guest of honour and Bernie
made a bee-line for him. Again more introductions. I
wondered, what do you say to an ambassador and his

wife. The PR manual had omitted this slight detail.

As if sensing my discomfort the ambassador's wife started to inform us of their previous evening's entertainment. She told us they had been to see *Spartacus*.

"Wonderful," I replied. "Isn't Kirk Douglas marvellous!"

"Oh No, No, DAAAARLING, . . . this was the BAAAAALSHOI BAAALLET."

Trap door please. And make it pretty damned quick!

A Nip around the World

Binge and Cringe

S ome look on my work and travel as very glamorous
indeed — the jet set life. Even my daughter Lynn,
aged seven. Recently she was asked in her classroom by
her teacher what her daddy did for a living.

"Oh," she replied, "my Daddy flies round the world
and pours people whisky. He also gives away free
ashtrays!"

THIS is what I do!? In a nutshell she had captured
the nature of marketing.

International markets, introducing the product and
then supporting it with a marketing budget. Embarking
on this career a well known local solicitor implied to me
that the constant travel would become a curse, a drudge,
much better being 'in your own bed at night'.

That has not happened with me. On the contrary, the movement, the meetings, the taste of different cultures, the feeling of seeing, organising, changing and operating outside your "safe" natural environment, albeit awkward, difficult and sometimes dangerous, is thrilling. BUT you must not let it become a drug.

It can be a very lonely occupation. You virtually live out of a suitcase. A recent trip in March involved eight nights away. A long drive from Scotland to Barcelona via Bordeaux and Andorra. 3500 miles in total, 11 fuel stops, 12 shirts, 3 suits, 24 music cassettes and 5 hotel changes.

You become disorientated and wonder where you are sometimes. Simple things like awakening in the morning and wondering where the loo is? It was somewhere else the night before, and the night before that.

My most embarrassing moment typifies this point. As with most business conducted abroad it is usual and customary for the host country to entertain the visiting party. It is bad manners not to accept this hospitality, regardless of the fact that all you want to do, in many cases, is crash out and sleep.

We had conducted a whisky tasting in one of

Barcelona's famous jazz clubs, La Cova Del Drac. It had started at five in the afternoon and went on until eleven.

About one hundred and fifty people visited, including trade press, shopkeepers and publicans. I talked and talked until hoarse. When the last left we set off and dined in a lovely traditional Spanish restaurant. It was the first time I had eaten raw flaked cod on a bed of tomatoes soaked in olive oil. Different and delicious.

There was a crowd of about fifteen sales men and women. That is a big round of drinks! I think as Scots abroad we overcompensate in buying rounds due to our unfair stigma of 'meanness'.

We concluded in an Irish bar, the time was now 3.00am. Bed beckoned at last! The hotel was four star — The Balmoral on the Vista Augusto No5. Quite posh.

This hotel was the fourth change of address in five days. I awoke at 4.00am bursting for 'a leak'. The front door of my room was adjacent to the loo.

I seriously needed to decant some Guinness. I grappled with the front door. Emerging outside, nude, I expected to see the usual toilet accessories. In this dazed state of semi-consciousness, I discovered that I was now on the landing. The door clicked locked behind me. Hells Bells! The nearby lift hummed to the tune of an ascending party.

F★★★! Do I run? No that's streaking! How do you get yourself out of that and survive? . . .

Such matters apart, my visit to Barcelona was a touching experience. The last time had been thirty two years before as a small boy of seven. I was with my parents (now deceased) and brother John.

I vaguely remembered having our photographs taken outside the famous Gothic cathedral. I knew that somewhere in an old suitcase that photograph existed. My brother and I had stumbled across it many years before. The cathedral is one of the most beautiful I have seen, a hallowed place, reaching upwards, as if to heaven.

It was easy to light two candles. On leaving I asked a passer-by to take my photograph. When returning home I hunted religiously for the original.

the original found — with parents in 1963, aged 7

not far off the same spot in 1995

Whisky expedition 1994

My trip to the United States began early in the morning of Friday 22nd April 1994. Snow flurries in the glens accompanied me on my journey south from Glenfarclas Distillery in Speyside to Glasgow Airport. I was excited by the prospect of what lay ahead.

This was not just a regular trip to the States. Normally I would go out to meet our distributor, or attend an exhibition — but this day I was on a singular and unusual mission.

The American Airlines flight to Chicago left punctually from Glasgow at lunchtime and I arrived at 3.30pm (local time) in Chicago, on the shores of Lake Michigan.

John Grant, who owns Glenfarclas and is my boss, had already arrived there earlier from Tokyo, and had hired a car for our outward journey.

The weather, in contrast to Scotland, was uplifting with a cloudless sky and warming sun. We headed south on Route 57 in the direction of Memphis and stayed overnight in Effingham, Illinois.

This small city was famous for printing. I later learned that both *Vogue* and *Playgirl* magazines are printed there!

The reason we were visiting Effingham was to meet one William Shrive. He had recently written to the distillery to explain his extraordinary find.

Just after prohibition had ended in the late 1920s, the bottling company of JG Thompson & Co Ltd, The Vaults, Leith had shipped out fifty wooden cases of Glenfarclas Malt Whisky. The importer in the States at that time was H Albrecht and Company, East St Louis, Illinois. In 1936, William Shrives' father, an engineer, purchased six cases.

Now one might have presumed that whisky of this quality, arriving in a recently 'dry' country, would have been quickly consumed. Remarkably, three unopened cases remained until 1968. From that date onwards, the stock diminished — but not completely. On this trip to the States we were going to pick up the last unopened wooden case, plus the last single bottle!

We met the jolly William Shrive the next morning at our hotel. A sprightly, cheerful man of 76, he was determined to carry in the case himself!

He placed the wooden case of twelve bottles on a table top in the hotel foyer. We instinctively knew this was the genuine article. It had all the import/export markings and each bottle was wrapped in wax paper. What a marvellous find!

I went on to interview Mr Shrive, who told me that he was born in 1918 in Belleville, Illinois. His father had hailed from Berwick, Pennsylvania, and his mother's ancestors from Frankfurt, Germany.

I asked him if he had any connection with Britain. He told me that his father had been an engineer and had worked in London on the Bakerloo–Waterloo railway line between 1905 and 1906.

William Shrive had followed his father in the

Effingham Illinois — (l–r) the author, William Shrive, and
John Grant of Glenfarclas

engineering tradition, eventually becoming president of
the Sterling Steel Casting Company of Cahokia in
Illinois.

During the Second World War he was an officer in
the Navy, affiliated with Higgins Industries, who built the
famous Uercha 100 foot PT or beach landing craft. I
pointed out to him that the fiftieth anniversary of D-day
was being celebrated in Europe in a few months' time.
The interview ended. After much hand shaking and good
wishes, we went our separate ways.

Our way was further south. In addition to picking
up this rare case of whisky, we had also come to the
States to attend the USA's largest 'spirits' convention —
the Wine and Spirit Wholesalers of America. This show,
which lasts five days, moves around the main American
cities on an annual basis. This year the venue was New
Orleans, which was where we were now heading.

The case was secured in the boot of the car for its
journey on to New Orleans. It was now midday and the
sun was beating down.

We made our way south from Illinois, a state almost
Dutch-like in its flatness, with a concentration on large-
scale agriculture. As we passed through Kentucky and

onto Interstate 55 toward Memphis, the countryside gradually changed to rolling hills and meadows. Memphis was 'full' that evening so we had to plump for an airport hotel.

Starting early the next morning, we left the city via Elvis Presley Boulevard and 'Graceland'. It was about 7.30am but already the sun was warming.

As we continued south through Tennessee and Mississippi the roadside grew lush, with mile upon mile of grass and evergreens. We crossed over the Tallahatchie River, desperately trying to remember whether it was Billy Joel, Billie Joe or Billie Jean that had jumped off the famous bridge!

Entering Louisiana around lunchtime the countryside again changed, becoming more Mediterranean in appearance. Pine groves and creepers, honeysuckle and 'thistles' predominated here. The sky was alive with swallows. A violent storm must have passed recently — many of the mature trees had been snapped like matchsticks.

We arrived in a busy and balmy New Orleans about four in the afternoon. In two days we had travelled from Lake Michigan in the North to the Gulf of Mexico in the

South. Around one thousand miles.

It was time for a beer! Our newly appointed importer was located in New Orleans. It was Sazerac Inc Co, named after probably the first American Cocktail, the 'Sazerac Cocktail', and later the famous Sazerac bar.

John Grant and myself both had invitations that evening for the opening cocktail party of the WSWA convention, hosted by Sazerac, at the Sazerac Bar in the Fairmount Hotel. Here we planned to debut our recent whisky find!

The setting could not have been more appropriate. Before it moved to the Fairmount Hotel, the Sazerac bar, which first opened just after prohibition, was originally on the corner of Carondelet Street and Cambone, opposite the US Navy headquarters. In 1944 William Shrive of Effingham, Illinois, and recent owner of a very rare case of Glenfarclas whisky, had been stationed in New Orleans. He had worked out of the US Navy Headquarters, and had been a frequent patron of the Sazerac Bar, where he had regularly enjoyed a 'Sazerac Cocktail' — the recipe he had detailed to me during our interview the previous day. An auspicious coincidence! We quickly changed and made an appearance at the Sazerac bar, 'case' in hand.

The trade were amazed. The press loved it. The malt whisky equivalent of the Dead Sea Scrolls!

The following week, this old and revered case of Glenfarclas travelled Club Class — with its own seat — on its British Airways flight from Atlanta to Gatwick.

It had sat undisturbed in a cellar in Illinois for nearly sixty years before returning to the distillery in Scotland from whence it came. John Grant described it as "a most exciting whisky find". But dare we open it!

John Grant presents a bottle to
Peter Bordeaux of Sazerac Inc, New Orleans

A Nip around the World

"Cities in the Sky"

This was my first round-the-world airline ticket. The first stage was London–Hong Kong — Cathay Pacific, Terminal 3, Heathrow at 6.00pm, 747 Jumbo Jet.

I sighed with relief at the sparsely populated departure lounge. The flight was going to be twelve hours long and I was travelling economy class. On entering the aircraft I quickly assessed and then 'proclaimed my territorial rights!'

The best option on a half empty 747 is the central rows of four seats. That way the armrests can be folded up and you have a reasonable bed. In fact, this option, if you can get it, is preferable to business class. To protect your bed from 'predators' you have firstly to assume your position in the *second* seat in. Once this is achieved you quickly spread out magazines, books, CDs etc into the adjacent seats. This reduces the risk of losing your bed. Finally, if a predator starts to eye up your 'park bench' you either give him or her a filthy stare, or blow them a kiss.

This is the life of a HOBO on a JUMBO!

It still remains a mystery to me how this squat, fat aircraft does the job? But what a job it does. The cabin lights were dimmed, the engines droned on, the time was now 11.15pm and the flight chart indicated we were passing over the Arabian Sea, 35,000 feet up at 512mph. I tried to relax and wondered again at this technological marvel.

Dinner had passed with some pleasant wine, a press of the button on the armrest would bring a smiling hostess offering a nightcap. I felt strangely content and at peace. I wondered how many people at this moment were on a Jumbo, in their own 'little cities in the sky'.

Our agent in the Far East is Richard Paine. He met me on arrival in Hong Kong and proved, along with his Japanese wife, to be cordial hosts. Arriving during the holiday weekend it was difficult to meet any customers.

However the real reason for visiting this area was to look at other brands of whisky and how they are packaged and marketed towards the Chinese and Japanese tastes.

I did have some free time and enjoyed very much taking the Peak trolley car up to an astounding view over Hong Kong harbour. The Star Ferry across the harbour was compulsory to the visit! My greatest pleasure however was two lovely nights in the Hong Kong Hilton, a pleasure which cannot be repeated as it will shortly be bulldozed to make way for more profitable office accommodation.

Richard departed with me the following day on the Cathay Pacific flight to Taiwan. It was surprising that a 747 was being used for such a short flight. However it was going on to Tokyo and the passenger numbers in this part of the world are much greater than in Europe.

As the flight was about to take off Richard began a conversation with me, explaining that he had Irish-Scottish connections. In fact the name Paine coming from the Irish, pagan.

The engines started to roar and the Jumbo began its long take off from the harbour runway at Hong Kong. You think it is never going to lift, but surely and steadily the nose begins to rise, the features transform from an ugly duck to a graceful swan — up, up and away.

As if given a cue from Richard I started to explain how most Scots have Irish ancestry and that the first settlements on the West coast of Scotland hailed from Ireland. The Celtic connection.

I further explained that part of the origins of early Scottish Christianity were to be found on the island of Iona. I told him that in the Autumn of last year I had visited Iona with a friend. We discovered that Iona was not only regarded as a religious settlement with the monastery, but also that the caves of this small island were the ancient burial chambers of the early Scottish kings.

The main purpose of my visit to the Far East was to look at packaging from the point of view of developing a whisky product in a very upmarket presentation. As this market is mainly gift orientated and expensive, the packaging must look the part. It is a bit like the French perfumery trade, where the bottle and presentations are exquisite, very expensive and selling a style or dream.

For the past two days Richard and I had been looking at the various competing brands and trying to come up with a novel idea. We were searching for a brand name, with a story, Scottish in theme, regal if possible, Celtic and historical.

We had talked of Iona, first Scottish settlements, early burial sights of kings, Celtic origins, ancient ways. We started to bounce names off each other — Royal Iona, Iona Mist, Isle of Iona, Kings of Iona . . . And then as if in unison, we both blurted out . . . IONA ROYAL! Then added an E to form IONA ROYALE.

Tokyo was the last stop on this leg of the tour. The impressions of this city were left clearly in my mind.

For a major city it was remarkably clean — I have not ever seen so many clean and polished cars. The taxis were immaculate with seat covers in white lace. The drivers wore white cotton gloves. They could operate a handle from the front which automatically opened the left or right rear doors, thus ensuring the passenger alighted pavement side, with no danger to themselves or the taxi door from passing traffic.

A bit different to New York!

Cherry blossom, pink and white gave the city a country wedding effect as the breeze caught the light blossoms, making them drift like confetti. Twenty million people live here with a further twenty million coming in daily to work.

I was curious at the numbers of Japanese going around with surgical facemasks. I imagined some huge communal medical operation about to be enacted. Later I was told that pollen levels were high, thus the masks. I also learned that if you have a cold it is customary to don the mask, reducing the spread of germs. Very social minded I thought, but discovered it also had economic reasons too . . . to reduce loss of productivity!

I had been well briefed to the etiquette here, especially at business meetings. The bow, the exchange of business cards with amazed expressions.

The bowing concerned me greatly. For some reason I could not get out of my mind a recent Rowan Atkinson Mr Bean TV sketch. In this comic scene Mr Bean portrayed a butler in a famous London hotel. The event was a Royal premier performance. The staff in their penguin suits are in line, Mr Bean included, awaiting the Royal visit. As they wait patiently they practice bowing and curtsying. Mr Bean seems to have got the bowing motion perfect.

However on being presented to the Queen Mother

he bows so quickly and with so much force that he 'head butts' the dear lady, who then falls unconscious to the floor. I thought of this sketch constantly at our first meeting with a Japanese company but prevented giving anyone a 'head butt' or 'Glasgow Kiss' as it is affectionately known in Scotland.

With our appointments concluded we headed back on the subway. I was impressed by the 'foot braille' on the walkways to assist the blind in directions.

At this time the subway was heavily policed due to terrorist gas attacks. I shivered when we passed Shinjuko station where twelve had died only days earlier. I left Narita Airport Tokyo the following day, at lunchtime on the 22nd.

The flight to Detroit was thirteen hours long, but arrived the same day, the 22nd, just before lunchtime. Of course crossing the dateline give you an extra half day, you arrive before you have left! A very weird feeling. You certainly do not feel half a day younger, more like a month older!

A Nip around the World

Special Agents

One of the prerequisites in developing an international brand is to build up a network of agents. This can take many years to achieve and is built up on trust. It is a constant task, keeping contact, feeding information, keeping faith, building trust. But it works to mutual advantage.

With few exceptions our distributors are family owned companies. It is simply not economic sense to have your own office and personnel placed in an overseas market, unless your sales are very significant indeed. Even then you may not have the same degree of market knowledge as a homegrown company.

I find from this, that we have a kind of common bond with our agents. We communicate easily on most occasions.

One company with which we have done business abroad for probably the longest is Mähler-Besse of Bordeaux. This is a charming company with a wonderful history. The jewel in the crown must be the Chateau and vineyards of Palmer. (Pronounced PALLL-MERRRR.)

It lies in the famous Margaux region of Bordeaux. The main body of the vineyard is directly to the south of Chateau Margaux and on a small plateau, the first of several that ripple away from the estuary of the River Gironde. Here the soil is at its most refined, the climate perfect.

The name derives from a Major General Palmer, of the British Army, who settled in the region, in the early nineteenth century.

It was previously known as Chateau de Gasq, from the family of that name, who also owned part of the nearby Leoville estate. On the 16th June 1814, the widow of Blaise Alexandre De Gasq sold the Chateau to the Major General, who had just inherited a vast fortune.

Legend has it that the despondent widow met the General in a stagecoach en route from Paris to Lyon — a long harsh journey in those days. However by the time they had reached their destination a deal had been struck.

the attractive Chateau Palmer which overlooks its own vineyards

The passing years were to prove however that Major General Palmer had little business acumen and would have been better suited to soldiering.

Just before the 1855 classification, the Perrier family acquired the property and built the present Chateau.

In 1938, the estate was divided and came into the hands of a Civil Company, the main shareholders of which are the descendants of Frederick Mähler who had founded the firm of Mähler-Besse following the marriage to Marguerite Besse in 1905.

Today Mähler-Besse is a highly respected international organisation associated with products of excellence, not least of which are the fine wines of Chateau Palmer.

The fairy tale Chateau is a typical mid nineteenth century family mansion. Proud and magical from the outside with elegant conical towers and intricate balustrades.

Inside on the ground floor there are two main rooms — the salon and the dining room. These are truly gorgeous with the focal point in the salon being the marble fireplace.

Now beautiful ornate fire surrounds are not uncommon in grand houses of this period, but what makes this so unusual is that immediately above it, on the line of the lintel, is a tall window. This provides an open view down through an avenue of trees onto an endless lawn. The smoke from the fire directly below is ducted away on either side to allow an uninterrupted view. This magnificent feature gives the impression of a constantly changing watercolour throughout the seasons.

The Chateau, like many others was occupied by the German army during the last war, and the upper floor, which is locked off, remains chillingly unchanged since their leaving those many years ago.

Bordeaux is rightly famous for its splendid wines, but it also acts as host, on a biennial basis to VINEXPO. This is the world's major wines and spirits exhibition and its shop window. In 1993, 2100 exhibitors from 42 countries were present, with Japan, Luxembourg, Romania, Sweden, Bolivia and Moldavia being represented for the first time. In 1991, 55,682 visitors from 93 countries, came to VINEXPO for five days of business contacts and meetings.

It is usual for our company during VINEXPO to host a dinner or lunch at Chateau Palmer. We invite the trade press, our overseas agents, their wives or husbands, girl or boyfriends, and generally anyone who has helped the brand name over the past few years. It is very effective and good public relations and a thank you from the company.

I remember well my first visit to Chateau Palmer and it has a lasting impression. We had decided to host a Scottish theme evening for around eighty guests. A nice size.

The choice of menu for dinner was to be typical and included haggis. For the uninitiated this food item is traditionally the stomach-sack (empty) of a sheep, stuffed with oatmeal (coarse flour) and usually the less expensive cuts of meat. It is often highly spiced with pepper and is delicious served with neeps (swedes) and tatties (potatoes). Ideal for the long cold Scottish winters.

Every January it takes on a hallowed role the length and breadth of Scotland as Chieftain of the Pudding Race in the celebrations to Robert Burns, the renowned Scottish poet.

We had taken several 'haggi' with us for the dinner, and had given our enthusiastic French chef what we thought were clear instructions. Haggis is usually boiled in water in its 'bag' for around thirty to forty minutes, depending on its weight.

Confusion must have occurred because our dear chef had decided to sauté all five haggis together, discarding their outer skins. Quite quickly thereafter the haggis started to dry out, turn golden, then brown, then started to smoke and stick to the base of the enormous pan.

"Monsieur Malcolm, Monsieur Malcolm, come quickly, we have *tres grande problem*," wailed the chef. By now a bluish smoky hue was drifting through to the dining room where the guests were starting to arrive.

It is customary in Scotland to accompany haggis with a dram (measure) of fine malt whisky. In fact many add whisky before cooking, to enhance the flavour. Others pour a little over the warm haggis as a sauce.

One of the products our company produces is a cask strength whisky at 60% alcohol by volume or 105 degrees proof! This is whisky at its natural strength as drunk in the eighteenth century. Many food producers add '105' Glenfarclas to give a distinct whisky flavour to items as diverse as marmalade, mustard, honey, toffee and naturally enough, tinned haggis!

By now mayhem was breaking out in the tiny kitchen as the haggis slowly became cremated. Thinking of saving the day, I grabbed a bottle of '105' and dashed into the kitchen. I then quickly dispersed the entire contents into the deep pan.

WHOOSH! — an enormous blue flame rocketed skywards. I imagined the whole Chateau going up in smoke as the turbo charged pot ignited.

Front page PR I thought, what publicity! Pity about the job though! Incredibly as swiftly as it had occurred the flame subsided and disappeared like a genie. It left the most delicious aroma. The darkened haggis looked miraculously refreshed by its experience.

"Monsieur Malcolm, Monsieur Malcolm, *Tres BIEN, Tres BIEN*," cried the excited chef. "*FLAMBE HAGGIS D'ECOSSE!*"

•

A mixed bag of international journalists, wine writers, buyers from airlines, Masters of Wine, merchants and wine snobs gathered for the second evening of wine tasting in the magnificent cellars of Chateau Palmer. Ten large tables were set out, all covered with immaculate white linen. On each table sat fifteen bottles of Palmer with ten gleaming glasses allocated to each.

Each taster was given a card listed one to fifteen with the appropriate definitions of colour, nose, taste and most importantly vintage. All the bottle labels were obscured, so thus we were literally tasting 'blind'.

Previous experience had revealed that it was likely that the younger vintages would be served first with the older 'creme de la cremes' last. A vertical tasting. So it began.

As the tasting neared the end the orgasmic adulations became louder and louder. There was much sucking and gurgling through clenched teeth. From number ten onwards I had forsaken the spittoon for my stomach. One knew this was old Palmer and with my instinctive Scottishness simply could not bear to spit it out.

I thought I had been guzzling surreptitiously. But I had been observed On the last glass I sucked, with much Oohing and Aahing, then swallowed the liquid pleasure. "This is not the Etiquette," he accused, with booming voice, nose high in the air. "One simply does not swallow."

I felt like a small boy being caught taking a bite from an apple from under the school desk. I flushed a little. Regaining my composure I insisted that my Scottish blood could not see such fine wine going to waste. A few giggled around the table.

"Anyway," I exclaimed, "given that the last five wines were 1979, 1978, 1975, 1967 and 1966 Chateau Palmer, it was simply irresistible." He smiled arrogantly at my obvious confidence at guessing the correct vintages.

"Well then, let's see," said Mr Haughty as he leered at our group. The vintages were duly announced and my card was vintage perfect. All fifteen.

The group stopped giggling. Mr Haughty glared at my card, and could not contain his bewilderment. How could this uncivilised creature from the wilds of Scotland have been so accurate, he must have wondered?

I did not have the heart, nor the inclination to tell him that we had been accidentally invited to the previous evenings tasting, and that tonight had been a precise re-run!

diary of a whisky salesman

The Whisky Trail

July is one of the quietest months in the year for distilleries. In fact many at this time of year have their traditional silent season, a period of planned maintenance. Also malt whisky sales tend to slump a little during the hotter months.

In contrast to this sleepy period, an influx of whisky enthusiasts lands in on the Speyside area. This is the home of the famous Malt Whisky Trail. From all corners of the world they come.

Probably the most famous destination of all is Glenfiddich Distillery. During my studies at university I worked for most of my holiday time with this company. Along with Glenfarclas and Glenlivet, they pioneered the distillery visitor centre, beginning in the late 1960s. I was employed as a tourist guide to show visitors round the distillery and explain the benefits of malt whisky. There were only six guides then. Today they have a staff of more than forty, and look after over 120,000 visitors annually.

I enjoyed my experience with Glenfiddich very much and could not help but marvel at their PR and marketing skills. My interview for this job was memorable. How could I forget it? It shaped my career!

I sat waiting to be called into the distillery manager's office. Faded photographs of founding fathers adorned the whitewashed walls. An old black rubber mat with *Grants Standfast — The Spirit of the Empire* in bold wide letters, gripped the linoleum floor.

I felt a little bit intimidated by the weight of tradition, but was put at ease by the gentleman who greeted me. This was Major George Coombe.

A very warm man, steeped in army tradition, a little eccentric with his checked shirt and regimental tie, Black Watch tartan trews and highly polished brogues. He must have taken a dram or two of whisky, as his nose was purple red with those tell-tale veins that look like a road map!

George Coombe at the Glenfiddich Distillery

He seemed very interested in my upbringing. In a nutshell I was brought up in a small family grocers. We had to work, serving customers, most Saturdays throughout the teenage years.

The Major implied that this experience in dealing with the general public would be valuable as a tourist guide. I imaged he thought I was good with people, which I felt at the time was a correct assumption.

Years have passed since then, fifteen in fact. I met the Major last year, months before his death. He was of the old school, a gentleman, always interested in his staff, his troops. A bit like an old fashioned teacher.

On that last, chance meeting at Inverness Airport I observed his failing features It reminded me of my father during his last cancer months. A yellowish ivory complexion, shrunken cheeks.

"Major Coombe," I exclaimed, "do you remember me?" Despite his deathly appearance, two very blue eyes twinkled in recognition.

"Why, my dear Malcolm."

It was an awkward conversation at first. He knew,

that I knew, he was going to die soon. I changed the course of the conversation into something more 'army barracks'.

"Major Coombe, you old bugger. Do you realise that *you* are to blame for my present career in this awful whisky industry?" I said jokingly. I referred to that interview at Glenfiddich many moons ago.

"Why yes, dear chap, and haven't you done so well since."

I felt proud at such recognition. He reminisced.

"I remember the interview well, Malcolm. What impressed me most was your size."

Size? Size??? "What do you mean, Size?" I questioned. Was it not my 'charm' and experience with the public, I thought?

"Did you not realise Malcolm?" quipped the Major, "I needed a strapping young lad to help me carry the heavy whisky boxes into the visitor centre, to restock the shop. My back was giving me hell at the time!"

•

Many thousands visit the Malt Whisky Trail every year. Half of all the malt whisky distilleries in Scotland are in Speyside. Famous brand names are prevalent on sign posts along the seventy mile journey.

Research has proven that few visitors actually do the whole trail, preferring to drop in on just one or two distilleries. This is a shame as all offer superb highland hospitality and a 'wee dram'. And each is unique. Although you do need a designated sober driver for this task!

Distillery visitor centres can be found in everything from converted old mills and original maltings to a former railway station.

CARDHU DISTILLERY, Knockando

Originally the site of illicit distilling until 1924 when the founder, John Cumming, took out a licence. His wife, Helen would warn crofters in surrounding hills of approaching excisemen looking for illicit stills by flying a red cloth from the barns. The blend of Johnny Walker RED label has its roots here.

Within the vistor centre you can look up from below at what used to be the malt kiln. Cardhu in Gaelic means 'black rock'. Although hidden from the road by a fold in the hill the distillery is easily found and lies just outside the village of Knockando.

(Owned by United Distillers)

GLENFARCLAS DISTILLERY, Ballindalloch

This is one of the few remaining independent
family distillers. Since 1836 five generations of the Grant
family have distilled a premium malt whisky.

After your guided tour of the distillery you can
relax and enjoy your 'dram' in the unique ambience of
the 'Ship's Room'. The panelling in here originates from
the famous *Empress of Australia* ocean liner. The present
chairman, George Grant on hearing of the sale of this
fine panelling, promptly made an offer. This was
successful and the feature was incorporated into the
visitor centre as it was built in 1973.

(still family owned)

GLEN GRANT DISTILLERY, Rothes

This is another distillery with its roots steeped in illicit practice. What I find most curious is the lovely orchard behind the visitor centre. Further up you would come to a rock face with a bubbling burn running alongside.

Embedded into the rock is an old metal safe. The previous owners liked a little tipple here as inside there is a bottle of Glen Grant and two glasses. Water is at hand, but you need that KEY! Glen Grant is the biggest selling malt whisky in Italy.   (Owned by Seagram)

DALLAS DHU DISTILLERY, Forres

This area is famous for Shakespeare's Macbeth. He met the three witches here!

It also inspired Roy Williamson of the popular folk music duo, The Corries to write Scotland's other national anthem, *Flower of Scotland*.

Although the distillery is no longer in production it is custom built for visitors to wander round at their own pace. This was the last distillery to be built in the nineteenth century and is a lovely 'time capsule' of the distiller's craft.   (managed by Historic Scotland)

GLENFIDDICH DISTILLERY, Dufftown

This is PR and Marketing finely tuned. The first whisky ran from the stills on Christmas Day 1887. The malt barn serves now as the vistor centre where you can enjoy your dram after a superb tour.

Glenfiddich is the only Speyside distillery to have a bottling hall on site and on view to visitors. This is a truly global brand still family owned.

the still house, Glenfiddich

STRATHISLA DISTILLERY, Keith

Established in 1786, this is the oldest operating distillery in the Highlands. The stonework is exquisite as are the two finely crafted 'pagodas'. An old water wheel creates a relaxed atmosphere. Another global brand has its origins here, Chivas Regal.　　(owned by Seagram)

THE GLENLIVET DISTILLERY, Glenlivet

This is one of the world's famous malt whiskies and it alone can use 'The Glenlivet' name for branding. It is set in beautiful rolling hills where the River Livet forms.

George Smith the founder had the foresight to see the demise of illicit distilling and was one of the first to take out a licence to distill on his farm in 1823. As production grew he and his son John Gordon opened a new distillery on the present site at Minmore Farm in 1858.

The early days of 'legal distilling' had their dangers. Smugglers grew envious of Smith's distillery and threatened to burn it down. Being a resolute man, and with the aid of a pair of hair trigger pistols he saw off the threat. These pistols can still be seen on show at the Glenlivet Reception Centre today. (Owned by Seagram)

SPEYSIDE COOPERAGE, Craigellachie

In the heart of the malt whisky country lies this famous Cooperage. It is here that you can discover the time-honoured art of making oak barrels.

All of these vistor centres have fine gift shops. Up-to-date information on visiting times and how to get there can be obtained from the tourist office in Elgin. My tip is to give yourself a couple of days, find yourself a good B&B, avoid July and August, and find that elusive driver!

Speyside Cooperage visitor centre

A Perfect Place

First Witch
When shall we three meet again?
In thunder, lightening, or in rain?
Second Witch
When the hurly-burly's done,
When the battle's lost and won.
Third Witch
That will be the set of sun.
First Witch
Where the place?
Second Witch
Upon the heath.
Third Witch
There to meet with Macbeth.
later . . .
Macbeth
So foul and fair a day I have not seen.
Banquo
How far is't called to Forres . . .

(From Shakespeare's Macbeth)

What a very British trait it is to talk so much of the weather. Forres is where these three hags supposedly met, to talk not only on the weather, but on a much grander level. The fate of Scottish kings.

Well I don't know any Scottish kings, but when anyone asks me from where I come, I usually inflict on them the importance of Forres which today is a sleepy market town in the north-east of Scotland.

I should have been born Elgin, but no. On that February night in 1956 my father set off for the twelve mile journey from Elgin to the Leanchoil Maternity Hospital in Forres. It was bitterly cold with snow flurries. He must have cursed my mother's oversight, at not giving her dates to the maternity ward in Elgin. It was full that night.

Halfway through the journey, the Austin A40 hit black ice, landing sideways in a farm ditch. No harm was done except to my father's pride, and mother 'and I' made the journey in time, thanks to a passing Bluebird bus. I can't help thinking now, that this slightly undignified entrance into the world, would be 'par for the course'.

My earliest recollections as a toddler must be of our

beach days in nearby Hopeman. This is a small fishing
village on the Moray Firth coast, between Kinloss and
Lossiemouth. It has the most wonderful sheltered beach
with crags and pools, fine sparkling white sand like that
found in old-fashioned hour glasses. Along the grassy
dunes stands proudly a procession of brightly coloured
beach huts.

How is it as a child you remember the summers as
deliciously hot? Regardless of the weather it was on
Wednesday and Sunday afternoons with picnic hampers
stowed we made our way off to the beach. Mother,
Father, Grandma, Uncle Jimmy, Auntie Jessie, brother
John and myself — all piled into the burdened Austin.

Europe goes on holiday in August. A time to avoid
airports, ferry terminals and motorways! I stay at home.
Exactly what has kept me here in the north-east of
Scotland for quite so long still puzzles me. It is an area
where I have grown up, a place and people I know well.

It is a place of exceptional natural beauty. An
unspoilt coastline, lush fertile fields, pure fast flowing
rivers, rugged mountains, and vast pine forests.

Most of the world's famous malt whisky brands
come from this area. It is no coincidence, as the spring

water here is of the finest quality. The Japanese despite their innovative skills have been unable to emulate it. In fact they have given up trying to! Instead they have decided to buy up Scottish distilleries.

Like an artery, giving life blood to the region flows a very special river, the Spey. At 1500 feet, south-east of Creaga Chait, and five miles from the west shore of Loch Lagan, it forms. One mile from its source is Loch Spey.

It torrents down through Strathspey, one hundred and ten miles to the sea, descending rapidly from snow-capped mountains. This makes the River Spey the fastest flowing and some would say the most dangerous in Britain. Its beauty belies its hidden mysterious dangers, catching many anglers unaware. Powerful currents, slippery boulders leading to deep pools, combined with freezing snow-melt waters often lead over-enthusiastic fishermen to their doom.

Rubber chest-waders are stretched to their outer limits for the elusive sea-run salmon, the king of fish.

In Summer, with low water, it is difficult to imagine the gentle gurgling flow, sparking with sunlight and dusted with hatching flies, dank in moist aromas, to be anything like the powerful beast it is in Spring.

Yet the river is the lifeblood of the area. Soft and pure, dark as Irish Stout. Water of such fine quality, melting slowly as snow, filtering downwards through heather and peatbog and over an ancient granite base below. It is little wonder that the world's finest malt whiskies are created here.

My very first experience of a Speyside distillery was on just leaving school, awaiting my exam results. I worked at 'the peats' above the Glen of Rothes.

Peat is a compacted burning material, sodden and sponge-like in its natural bog. Dark raisin brown in colour, formed through time and the compression of decaying heather and fallen trees. It is heavy and back breaking work to cut by hand and then stack in loosely constructed pyramids to dry on a summer breeze.

Distilleries use peat in the final stages of malting to dry out germinated barley. Having a strong pungent mustiness when burnt it imparts an attractive smoked flavour to the grain.

At the end of a hot sweaty day a rickety dust-filled van would take you back to Elgin. But via Coleburn Distillery. Here in a cool yeasty room a very serious brewer would pour you a 'dram'. No bar measure, but a large splash of whisky from a large copper urn. This was cask-strength from a cellar, fiery yet remarkably smooth — a great combination.

Most Speyside distilleries are picturesque, blending as if genetically with the landscape. This was often on the insistence of the landowning lairds. They could never be allowed to look like factories or works.

The stillhouse of even the most commercial and efficient distillery has a certain magic. Its ambience is a time honoured thing, as if it has a special and almost religious quality. In Summer, through tiny windows, shafts of light illuminate the copper kettles as the sun goes down. The sweet fragrance of new whisky spirit, heavy on the air in bluish hues, catches the beams of light, like cigarette smoke in an old cinema. There is an earthy woody darkened atmosphere in the low cellars, as casks of whisky lie silent and sleeping, undisturbed, maturing through countless seasons.

An oriental touch confuses visitors, in the shape of strange 'pagoda' chimneys used in former times for malting.

Yet this very romantic rural Scottish scene belies the very international and commercial basis on which these communities depend. Marketing and sales gurus have placed the products of these remote malt whisky distilleries into the global market.

The larger organisations have a system of sales and distribution outlets scattered around the world. The smaller producers rely mainly on a web of agents who act as distributors, often with a portfolio of other spirits and wines.

The Scotch whisky industry has become particularly concentrated over the past fifteen years. Most family owned companies have sold out to the larger corporations. The big players — Guinness, Seagram, Grand-Met, and Allied must account for nearly seventy percent of production. There is also a growing trend towards overseas ownership, with Seagram the Canadian multinational typifying this. Also the French company Pernod-Ricard owns three distilleries and a growing Japanese interest is evident such as in Macallan-Glenlivet and in outright ownership of Tomatin near Inverness.

Hopeman beach eastwards curves round in a perfect crescent. Almost central to it runs a small stream to the sea. This forms from the Braemou spring. Formerly a well, this was the main source of Hopeman's drinking water, prior to the installation of a piped domestic supply.

Children in the last century were sent to fetch water home in the morning prior to starting school. In earlier more superstitious times babies were often bathed in its waters to offer protection against the 'evil eye'.

My father till he died mistakenly believed this stream to be an open sewer, and kept us well away as toddlers.

The bay finishes with a buttress of sandstone rock heavily pock-marked with erosion. Further east brings you to a very symmetrical 'Lego-land' of sandstone bricks, all the result of time and nature. Yet so orderly and almost man-made in appearance. Then suddenly the soft sandiness of the beach abruptly ends.

Strange sea sculptured stones stand defiantly against the lashings of winter storms. Pebble and shell coves are strewn with wave tossed debris — a beachcomber's paradise of old lobster creels, sea bleached fishermen's boots, oddly shaped polystyrene, fish boxes bearing their port of origin, wonderful crooked tree stumps.

Sandstone, golden-brown and soft, dominates here, built up in layers under great pressure over millions of years. Lovers of yesteryear have left their vows etched on the cliffs. Fulmars, herring gulls and terns scream and spit

— dare you disturb their broods. You come across high cliffs and little bays cushioned by prickly golden gorse. The air here in summer is powerfully perfumed by their fragrance.

Blueberries grow in abundance and lichens and clover make perfect companions of silver and purple. The remains of an old sandstone quarry bears witness to man's ravages of this rugged coastline, as if some giant had just tipped a barrow load of boulders over the edge. Most of the surrounding area has used this material for building, and although much softer than granite, it is much easier on the eye. The twelfth century cathedral in Elgin bears testament to this beautiful stone.

A good half hour's treck through the heavy opiate of gorse and whins takes you to Primrose Bay, a secret place. Worn and erratic smugglers' steps welcome you downwards. When the tide is out an immense expanse of pure white sand treats and entices you. All is still and peaceful, a perfect place.

At sunset, on an ebbing tide, the sea sparkles like effervescent champagne, and glints like diamonds. Further east and past Lossiemouth a turquoise almost Caribbean colour meets the eye, as fresh water meets salt. This is where the River Spey ends.

A Nip around the World

Trips

B ack to work with a vengeance! Christmas beckons!

September is one of the busiest months in my diary. Although the marketing plan for the run-up to Christmas has been formalised and agreed months earlier, the reality of it now appears in dreadful clarity. By far the most sales are made during this period.

As the nights darken, and frosts return with the approaching winter the warming taste of malt whisky takes on again its allure. The visitors to the Speyside area slowly depart as schools return for the Autumn term.

This is a time for visiting our European agents to 'sell in' for the coming gift season. A typical trip at this time is by car, crossing to Rotterdam via Hull by North Sea Ferries. From Scotland I find this the most practical, rather than the long haul down to Dover and the awful M25.

The ferry company is very jolly, and tries hard to make the overnight crossing a pleasant and comfortable experience. But this round trip really begins and ends at Europort, Rotterdam. Countries visited will include Holland, Belgium, Luxembourg, France, Austria, Germany, and returning back to Holland.

Europort is not the best first impression of the Netherlands. It resembles a never ending metallic landscape, the heart of the petro-chemical industry. In the air cling sickly oil vapours. This would be the wrong impression. Holland is delightful, and one of my favourite countries.

In the next ten days I will drive through eight European countries. The hours spent in the car can feel very lonely at times. On the plus side the agents in these countries make you feel very welcome.

The very fact of visiting by car from Scotland puts you in a strong selling position. The impression given is that I am visiting agents and customers individually, to make them feel more important. Good relations are the key to a healthy order book!

I observed this first during my time at Glenfiddich distillery. Their success in part must be due to their 'special relationship' with distributors worldwide. There was always a visiting sales team at the distillery. They were given an excellent induction course and also a little free time. A good team spirit was evident and it taught me the value of face to face contact with your customers.

A distributor or agent is your first and principal customer. You have to encourage and assist them. It is not good enough to sell someone a container of your brand of whisky on the other side of the world, and say, thanks a lot, and that's it

No, you have to assist with marketing and get that whisky to move. That is to move off the shelf. Then you will get another order. Many companies when exporting miss this simple but essential detail. It is the second order that counts!

On returning to Hull you are faced with a longish drive back up to Speyside. In just two weeks you observe harsh changes in the landscape.

Combine harvesters have been at work, the fields shaven to conscript stubble. Some of this has been scorched black like a devilish ritual, the air acrid.

The light is softer, the air crisper, falling leaves start to make driving conditions slippery. Arriving back to my apartment, late at night, the door pushes back what seems endless bills. Fifteen days of mail. It will wait. It has already.

I click on the heating, pour a dram, and fall asleep on the sofa. The joys and loneliness of a long distance whisky salesman!

Service

O ctober is my most favourite month. Despite the encroaching winter, which in the North of Scotland lasts well into May, it is a time which fills me with warmth.

The Christmas promotions and offers are now in place throughout the principal markets. The stock is in place and delivered. It is now the time to go out and meet the publicans, shopkeepers and wholesalers alike. I very much enjoy this contact and from the marketing view it is essential. To meet the real people who sell your products. Without their help and assistance your brand is dead. They have to be on your side.

Yet it is with some sadness that we see the seemingly terminal decline of the small independent off-licence. The UK and Europe-wide retail outlets continue into further concentration, freezing out the corner wine shop and smaller producers alike. Choice for the consumer becomes limited to a few international brands who pay generously for the privilege to be on a supermarket shelf. Service and the human touch all but disappear.

My father always believed in providing a superior service and 'something different'. He was a Master Grocer and salesman.

October always reminds me of my parents. They both passed on during this month, but I do not feel sadness at this time. Only warmth. Perhaps the following story captures the reasons for this.

In 1936, my grandfather, John Simpson left the local wines and spirits merchants of Gordon and MacPhail to set up shop on his own, but on a much smaller scale. He had been badly gassed in the first war and did not survive long enough to see his dream fulfilled. Grandmother carried on and coped admirably well, even during the difficult rationing years of the second war.

My father, Bill was stationed by Elgin, prior to D-Day. Here he met, and later married the woman who was to be my mother. He had worked, prior to enlistment, at a small Derbyshire brewery. So it seemed natural for him to take over the shop. Besides grandma's eyesight was failing dramatically and she eventually suffered total loss of sight. She was a strong woman who rarely let her handicap unnerve her and lived to 96.

My childhood and teenage years revolved very much around the shop. Brother John and I were 'merchandising' — stacking shelves, on Saturdays, while during the week furthering our education.

In teenage years, no rugby matches for us on Saturday afternoons, but the duties of van and 'message' boys. We did not however feel exploited as the extra pocket money had its bonuses — we both have excellent collections of LPs!

The shop prospered in the sixties as a rush of new produce became available to satisfy the demands of these boom years. Wonderful tinned products from Australia were the vogue. Pears, pineapples, peaches and apricots in the sweetest syrups, marketed by AJC Bartlett; sweet and dry Imperial Bounty sherry. I remember the entire front window dedicated to this former colony, with colourful posters of kangaroos and the Great Barrier Reef, with a large banner proclaiming, *Australia sends her best to*

Scotland. This was long before our entry into the European Community and its terrible trade implications for Australia and New Zealand.

The aromas in this small licensed grocers were a source of great nasal delight. Freshly ground coffee, perfumed teas, pungent unpasteurised cheeses, smoked ham and waxed mahogany worktops.

There was a white starchiness surrounding father in his gleaming overalls, and customers were served. It was a venue for socialising as well as buying. A little in the French style.

It must be difficult for young people of today to imagine. Perhaps the closest to this would be at a cheese counter in a supermarket. But imagine having all your groceries served to you like this. Also with the added bonus of continuous chatter — it took ages!

If you were a little infirm, you could have your 'messages' as they were called, delivered by a 'message-boy', on a bike — me. Consider this beside the experience of shopping today? In that era you were not simply customers, but friends too. Shopping was socialising. They tell me this will return.

There were two levels in the shop with the specialised wines and spirits on the upper level. This was father's stage. His theatre. Being thin and scrawny he would descend on the unsuspecting customer with his overalls flapping. The ladies loved this and teased him on his knowledge of wines. He never seemed to stick.

One of the dilemmas facing a small grocers at that time was stocking the wide range of up and coming wines, malt whiskies and cognacs. These were expensive by the case and had a serious effect on cash flow.

Father's great delight, when faced with a particularly different request for a Bordeaux wine, was to stall. His eyes rolled and he scratched his chin pondering. "I may, just may have one bottle left in the cellar", he would mysteriously imply to the anxious tweedy lady. He would make his way slowly to the back shop, his gait quickening, then out the back door, down the close and darting like a hunted ostrich he would disappear down into the nearby cellars of Gordon and MacPhail. They kindly allowed him a running tab.

He would initial the sheet and quickly return to his shop a little out of breath. Gathering his composure he entered full stage dusting this rare discovery.

"There my dear, just what you wanted."

She would smile affectionately at his great skill. We thought this was wonderful salesmanship, albeit a little underhand. We had no cellar.

"French Kissing"

I like the French. What a wonderful attitude to life they have. For the activity that most of us conduct three times a day multiplied by 365 times a year, yes they have got it right. Food and drink are treated with the utmost respect.

The 'lunch hour' does not exist in France. Try telephoning a wine company there, between 12 noon and 3.00pm. They also love malt whisky. So this for me has never been a difficult market, except on the waistline. Much has been written on the French, their eating habits and general lifestyle, but what has caught my interest recently is their greeting behaviour. Their kisses.

We were attending the World Travel Market — the travel trade's main international show, and it is held in London's Earls Court exhibition halls. This was our sixth year of attending. The Scottish Tourist Board stand, of which we were a part, stood directly opposite the French equivalent.

Whisky distilleries by their nature attract much overseas interest and many of the big brands have attractive Visitor Centres. Tourists come by car and coach in their droves, so thus the reason for being at this show.

The Scottish stand theme was a castle. Not the most original concept maybe, but it serves a useful purpose and is visually strong. The stand was constructed with the perimeter being formed into individual booths, with each representing a hotel group, visitor attraction, coach company and many other tourist related sectors.

The interior of the castle serves as a hospitality lounge, for entertaining clients. This year was particularly well done with the catering being provided by one of Scotland's top chefs.

I invited our French colleagues into this haven for a 'wee dram' and we were served Haggis Balls as an accompaniment! They were about the size of a large grape, deep fried in breadcrumbs with the moist haggis stuffing inside — they were delicious. I always treat this dish however with the utmost respect!

For a large part, the exhibition serves as a reinforcement of existing business, a chance also to show new products or services. Occasionally like fishing, you do catch something big. In fact exhibitions in general are a bit like this.

You present yourself and company at its best, with an attractive stand, colour photo shots, glossy literature. Some go over the top with free gifts and chances to win exotic holidays. But they are, in doing so, simply offering a kind of bait. If the fish, the new business is not there, all the expense and effort for these shows is fruitless. Yet, if you do not go out there, and cast your net, then for sure nothing will come your way.

Sometimes an exhibition is simply an exercise in good public relations. It is also a chance to meet old friends, colleagues and acquaintances. There is much smalltalk and hand shaking. The French however take these chance meetings a bit more seriously. They kiss each other profusely.

Their stand was 'manned' by some very beautiful ladies who sat in their respective booths. It was a bit of a tease to observe these lovely women being embraced by their French colleagues. Kisses on each cheek, sometimes twice, followed by a heartwarming hug.

Our eyebrows raised, not to mention our blood pressure! One lady however stood out from the rest. Alexandra!

She stood there tall and graceful. No jewellery at all. Just a tiny black dress and matching velvet shoes. I caught her eyes first, dark and smouldering.

Perfect eyebrows, small nose and pouting mouth in rich ruby red. Her hair was long, dark and silken with a gentle wave. Tiny curls clustered around her temples. The curves of her bosom were slightly pronounced and she had a tiny waist with legs that never seemed to end.

I looked away, turned and looked back. She performed exactly the same exercise and we caught each other's glance and embarrassment. This time however her lips turned upwards into the most gorgeous smile. The slight dimples in her cheeks deepened and I am sure I detected the slightest blush. Our eyes held for what seemed like eternity. Oh! I simply must greet this lady, I thought.

We continued our analysis of the French greeting process. Further observation revealed that on some occasions they kissed each other only once on each cheek.

Then on others, three times, starting from the left. The ultimate was four times finishing with a bear hug. It was a spectacle to observe.

I wondered to my colleague, "What is the etiquette here?" We both clearly wished to say hello to our French cousins, the Auld Alliance and all that! The answer was simple. Each section of the French stand was split into regions, and each lady had her name and region proudly labelled. That was the trick.

Quite simply the number of kisses related to their own particular region. For example Paris is two kisses and Dijon three. However only the French know this code!

On pondering on this later, I thought, would it not have been a good idea, from an international aspect of course, to have marked on their name badges a simple 'lip' symbol indicating the correct number of kisses? Perhaps even include this in the *Michelin* guide as essential information for the traveller?

I was told recently, in great confidence, that this code of conduct goes to the wind, if you really like the person. Great.

The show was a week earlier than normal this year.

This had no serious implications other than the fact that this year *Beaujolais Noveau* arrived on the French stand.

This is a strange custom that seems to be dying out slightly. Certainly in the North East of Scotland. I can remember, not so long ago, a kind of cavalier attitude in getting that first case into the county. How MGB sportscars would be driven through the night, to arrive, overburdened and overheated, in the 'wee small hours'.

Hats off to the French in marketing this very youthful product. It was good publicity. Personally I don't like it. This attitude, of course, has nothing to do with the fact that we have to mature our whisky for ten years, before we can sell it. No, I find it a bit harsh and squeaky clean on my palate. But still, when those lovely ladies opposite invited us for a 'taste', how could I decline?

The hospitality area in the French stand was done out, as if from a Monet scene. Typical in style to a French café terrace, with gingham tablecloths over round wobbly tables, wicker chairs, that sort of thing. Even that famous man with the beard was there. It was a gay atmosphere in the true sense of the word. You could have danced!

What struck me as curious however, was the back wall. It seemed to jar a bit with the overall ambience. This was a wall, perhaps ten metres long by four high. The scene was that of a battle, D-Day. Normandy 1944. The mural was constructed with cardboard cutouts of US marines. British troops, bombs exploding, aircraft above, amphibious landing craft, dead bodies, the works.

It would be the fiftieth anniversary of this historical event the following year and the Normandy region were promoting this as a tourist attraction.

Now, I am not in the least bit unpatriotic. My father had been there. Indeed in a bizarre way, I would not have been here at all, had it not been for this event. He was with an English regiment which had been moved and stationed in Morayshire, just one week prior to the landings. However just before leaving, he had gone out with his mates to a local dance, and met my mother.

Accompanying this mural were artifacts such as gas masks, flying jackets, old grenades and many fading photographs. I even scanned the latter hoping for a glimpse of my father. But, no, he had been just a common soldier.

There seemed to be a kind of theme around the mural as if it was saying "Yeah — we whipped them didn't we."

Yes we did, and rightly so. The world is better for it. But do we rub salt in the wounds? And for how long? I thought it was a bit insensitive. The German stand was just nearby.

I noticed Alexandra fidgeting and obviously uncomfortable. She recalled a scene, as told by her mother, who is half German. That had been a little bit difficult for her mother during the war — not being 'true blooded'. The story went on, that her mother as a child, had been playing in a poppy field, just outside Cologne, during the last months of the war. The air raid sirens went off and could be heard vividly in the distance. As a young child she panicked and started to run for no obvious shelter.

This was strictly against regulations as it attracted roving bombers. As predicted, this duly happened, but she reached a covey of trees just in time. But in sheer terror and only five years old. Strangely then, this scene behind us, had an eerie and nostalgic effect on both of us.

I thought, perhaps for a moment, that her grandfather could have been shooting at my father, but that was ridiculous. It made me wonder later, if the Scottish stand in 1995, would depict a mural from the Inverness region, on the 250th anniversary of the Battle of Culloden. This was when the English 'whipped' the Scots, and was the last real battle on British soil. Perhaps. But somehow, I doubt it!

But the Beaujolais was fresh, fruity, 'youthful', and went down a treat.

A Nip around the World

Köln in the Kilt

The German city of Köln was in chaos when I arrived. Much of the lower quarter was under water due to the Rhine breaking its banks. The temperature was 5 degrees below freezing, a penetrating intense cold.

I was in the city to assist with an in-store tasting in a luxury department store. My girlfriend, Sandra was joining me from Dijon and arrived later that evening. She had been born in Köln and was able in the evening, to show me some of the less well known parts.

Köln is a beautiful city and despite the floods was most definitely in a festive mood. Christmas was only four days away and choirs and street performers were in their element. The shops and stores glistened, the restaurants and bars bulging with custom. I noticed the tasteful effort which Germans put into their Christmas decorations. Exquisite use of greenery and natural foliage, as if truly taking the forest inside. It was also a nasal delight with pungent cinnamon, cloves, citric essences blended with the pine freshness of the conifers. The simple Christmas tree originates from pagan times in Germany.

It was normal procedure to don the kilt for such promotions, but it was a thought to go out unprotected in these freezing conditions. I also wore a heavy woollen coat, knee-length.

Now, on being fitted for the Scottish kilt, the kiltmaker takes his final length sizes from asking the customer to go down on his knees. The length of the cloth should in theory just touch the ground. The point I am trying to make is that if you wear a long coat with the kilt, all you see are bare knees and socks.

The in-store promotion went very well and so it should have, given the time of year. Sandra did some Christmas shopping while I was working and it was uplifting to meet her at the end of the day. It is hard work appearing enthusiastic all day. Please have some thought for those store and duty-free men and women who offer free tastings! It is much less glamorous than it looks.

We dined that evening in a very traditional German restaurant and despite the beautiful surroundings and delicious food, perhaps through tiredness or just a little too much wine, we quarrelled.

Sandra loves clothes, in particular underwear. Her French grandmother had instilled in her the need of a proper lady to be properly dressed underneath. My mother, on the other hand, taught me the importance of clean underwear, just in case we were knocked down by a passing bus, and taken to hospital! She would have been 'black affronted' (extreme Scottish embarrassment) were hygeine standards shown to be not so. For me I would rather NOT be knocked down and wear my underwear a second day!

After the second day of the promotion, and our quarrel, I decided to treat Sandra to some fine black lacy underwear - she would choose burgundy. We left the enbalming warmth of the store and into a crowded shopping precinct. A Peruvian band were playing Christmas hymns on the pan pipes. Haunting seductive music.

My knees started to flinch at the cold.

There was a little strip of unprotected flesh between the bottom of the coat and my kilt socks. Sandra laughed at the startled glances of the passing shoppers.

We ended up in the lingerie department of a vast store. There seemed to be no other male around. Do German men not buy sexy underwear for their girlfriends or wives at Christmas I thought?

Sandra began her selection. I became increasingly uneasy at the constant downward stares at my knees. The air was stifling, laced by a fragrant cocktail from the nearby perfumery department. I wanted OUT.

Eventually — how can she take so long? — she made her selection. At last I thought? But no, she had to try them on for size. I sat outside the changing rooms. Thank you store managers/esses for providing this little haven! We would gladly pay for a beer!

I heard my name called out by Sandra amid the throng of semi-naked women. A bra came flying outwards with instructions for the next size up. Dutifully I obliged, returning with the requested garment.

On entering into the booth area, bra in hand, I mistakenly took another's for Sandra's.

Two enormous black breasts confronted me, NOT Sandra's.

A cry broke out — "VERDREHEN" (meaning pervert in English). My German is not very good but I got the message! What me!? . . . bra in hand, long coat, bare knees, perspiring, manic eyes . . .NEVER!

"Sandra dear, let's get out of here," or words to that effect. Later we laughed till tears appeared on our cheeks. We had a better dinner that night . . . and she had her new burgundy underwear!

The image of the kilted Scot may appear to be being knocked here. This is not intended. Indeed it gives me great pride and pleasure to work abroad, at exhibitions or tastings and wear the national dress.

There are few countries which have such a strong dress image. You are instantly recognisable and believable as Scottish and I find that people warm to you almost immediately. When asked what is worn underneath, I always reply, "Nothing is worn underneath, everything is in perfect working order!"